Robert S. Duncanson

Landscape Painter

Celebrating BLACK ARTISTS

Robert S. Duncanson

Landscape Painter

CHARLOTTE ETINDE-CROMPTON AND
SAMUEL WILLARD CROMPTON

nslow Publishing
NY 10011
nslow.com

Published in 2020 by Enslow Publishing, LLC.
101 W. 23rd Street, Suite 240, New York, NY 10011

Library of Congress Cataloging-in-Publication Data

Names: Etinde-Crompton, Charlotte, author. | Crompton, Samuel Willard, author.
Title: Robert S. Duncanson : landscape painter / Charlotte Etinde-Crompton and Samuel Willard Crompton.
Description: New York : Enslow Publishing, 2020. | Series: Celebrating black artists | Includes bibliographical references and index. | Audience: Grades 7-12.
Identifiers: LCCN 2019004362| ISBN 9781978514775 (library bound) | ISBN 9781978514768 (pbk.)
Subjects: LCSH: Duncanson, Robert S., 1821-1872—Juvenile literature. | African American painters—Biography—Juvenile literature. | Landscape painters—United States—Juvenile literature.
Classification: LCC ND237.D77 E85 2020 | DDC 759.13 [B] --dc23
LC record available at https://lccn.loc.gov/2019004362

Printed in China

Photo Credits: Robert S. Duncanson – Photo Research by Bruce Donnola

Cover, p. 3 McCord Museum I-11978.1; pp. 8, 11 The Picture Art Collection/Alamy Stock Photo; p. 11, 34, 43 Library of Congress Prints and Photographs Division; pp. 18-19 Sally Anderson Archive Photos/Alamy Stock Photo; pp. 22-23 Fotosearch/Archive Photos/Getty Images; pp. 28-29 Detroit Institute of Arts, USA/Bridgeman Images; pp. 32-33 Minnesota Historical Society/Corbis Historical/Getty Images; p. 37 Print Collector/Hulton Archive/Getty Images; p. 39 Corbis Historical/Getty Images; p. 41 Universal History Archive/Universal Images Group/Getty Images; pp. 46-47 Art Collection 3/Alamy Stock Photo; p. 49 Time Life Pictures/The LIFE Picture Collection/Getty Images; pp. 50-51 Detroit Institute of Arts, USA/Gift of Mrs. Jefferson Butler and Miss Grace R. Conover/Bridgeman Images; pp. 58-59, 80-81 Art Collection 2/Alamy Stock Photo; pp. 60-61 Universal Images Group/Getty Images; pp. 62-63 Mead Art Museum, Amherst College, MA, USA/Gift of William Macbeth, Inc./Bridgeman Images; pp. 68-69 DEA Picture Library/De Agostini/Getty Images; p. 70 Historic Collection/Alamy Stock Photo; p. 73 Art Collection/Alamy Stock Photo; pp. 78-79 Sourced Collection/Alamy Stock Photo; p. 87 History and Art Collection/Alamy Stock Photo; p. 90 Pictorial Press Ltd/Alamy Stock Photo

Contents

Chapter 1

The Painter and the Poet

Robert S. Duncanson led a remarkable life. As a black man, he managed to become a world-famous artist in the nineteenth century, a time when African Americans were still enslaved. He started out as a house painter and then became a landscape painter, a career that took him all over the globe. He was said to be the first African American artist to visit Europe as well as the first to earn rave reviews from international critics. By excelling in the art world, he blazed a trail for other black artists to follow. This is what makes his story so special.

While much of Duncanson's life remains a mystery, his paintings are a reflection of his character and talent. His highly productive life deserves praise, but Duncanson's contributions to painting have largely been overlooked since his death roughly 150 years ago. In the twenty-first century, that's beginning to change, with institutions such as the Smithsonian, Hampton University, and the Los Angeles County Museum of Art all taking an interest in the man and his work.

This portrait of Robert S. Duncanson was taken after his rise to fame as one of the nation's most talented landscape artists and the first world-famous African American artist.

In 1865, however, Duncanson was so famous that the most influential people on both sides of the Atlantic Ocean knew his name. This included aristocrats such as Alfred, Lord Tennyson, the celebrated British poet.

The Inspiration for *Land of the Lotus Eaters*

In 1865, England was a world superpower. The capital city of London was not only a center of commerce and trade but also of the arts and sciences. Biologist Charles Darwin's theory of evolution had made him the star of the scientific community, and Tennyson's poetry had made him the darling of the literary community. For more than thirty years, Tennyson had turned out splendid work, with his "Charge of the Light Brigade" deemed a genuine masterpiece of art.

Viewed as shining examples of all that England did best, Darwin and Tennyson were revered in London. But both men much preferred their homes in the country to the city. Darwin lived in Kent, and Tennyson lived on the western side of the Isle of Wight.

There, Lord Tennyson welcomed Robert S. Duncanson, all because the two men shared a bond over a poem Tennyson had written thirty-three years earlier. He called it "The Lotos-Eaters," as it was based on the travels of Odysseus, the Greek hero who deceived the Trojans and led their city to fall. In the poem, Tennyson describes how the Greek sailors felt as they took in the Land of the Lotus-Eaters. He wrote:

A land of streams! Some, like a downward smoke,
Slow-dropping veils of thinnest lawn, did go;
And some thro' wavering lights and shadows broke,
Rolling a slumberous sheet of foam below.
They saw the gleaming river seaward flow
From the inner land; far off, three mountain-tops.[1]

The lotus blossoms seduce the Greek sailors. Captivated, the men declare their wish to remain in the region—perhaps forever. They prefer life on the shore, where they can rest, to life at sea, where they often sail through wind and rough waters.[2]

One day, Tennyson was pleasantly surprised to see a photograph of a painting that captured the scene he described in "The Lotos-Eaters." He discovered that the painter lived in Canada and wrote to him at once to congratulate him on his artistic vision. Addressing the letter to "one of my Canadian kinsmen,"[3] Tennyson praised the painting, saying it looked very much like he'd imagined the Land of the Lotus-Eaters to be. Moved by Robert S. Duncanson's work, he asked if the painter would visit Farringford, the Tennyson estate on the Isle of Wight.

Tennyson had written to Duncanson in 1864, but a year would pass before Duncanson made it to England. He arrived by way of Ireland, where two of his major paintings were exhibited in Dublin. His presence in London attracted a great deal of press, and it was nearly all because of his painting based on Tennyson's poem.

Today, Sweden's royal family owns the striking piece of art. *Land of the Lotus Eaters* is 53 by 89 inches (135 by 226 centimeters). The painting features a large landscape,

Tennyson's Error

Lord Tennyson made a mistake when he wrote to Duncanson. He referred to him as a Canadian because the image he saw of Duncanson's painting came from Canada. Though Duncanson had spent several years in that North American country, he was a New York-born American.

Tennyson's mix-up about Duncanson's nationality also begs another question: Did the poet realize he'd invited a man of color into his home? And would he have still extended the offer had he known beforehand?

A bust portrait of Alfred, Lord Tennyson, facing right. Robert S. Duncanson was so inspired by the poet's work he created a landscape painting based on it.

with lush tropical plants and brown soil in the foreground and snow-capped mountains in the background. The Greek sailors can be found in the painting's lower left corner. A group of brown-skinned natives presents them with the gift of lotus plants to induce them into a state of bliss and compel them to remain in the land forever.

Duncanson's painting does not match Tennyson's poem exactly, but it's similar enough for viewers to notice the resemblance. One way that Duncanson's painting differs from Tennyson's poem, however, is that it may allude to the US Civil War and slavery. The late art scholar Joseph D. Ketner, who studied Duncanson at length, argued that it is no accident that brown people serve the lighter-skinned Greeks in *Land of the Lotus Eaters*. Also, the painting portrays the Greeks as technologically advanced and the natives as unsophisticated.

Ketner asserted that *Land of the Lotus Eaters* is an allegorical painting. An allegory is a work of art—story, poem, painting, or other work—believed to have a secret political or moral meaning. Since Duncanson finished the painting in 1861, when the Civil War began, Ketner suggested that the dark-skinned natives represent African Americans, and the impaired, lotus-eating Greek sailors symbolize the ignorance with which many white Americans viewed race.[4]

Meeting Tennyson

It's unclear exactly when Duncanson visited Tennyson in 1865. The amount of time that has gone by since then is one reason the details remain unknown, but the fact that the poet routinely received distinguished guests is another.

Multiple Layers

Like most great art, *Land of the Lotus Eaters* can be read on several levels. One can, indeed, pick out much of what Joseph Ketner said about the painting–that the natives represent enslaved African Americans and the Greeks represent white Americans intoxicated by racism.

At the same time, *Lotus Eaters* can be enjoyed for what it is: a magnificent landscape painting. One British art critic declared, "The picture is full of fancy. It is a grand conception, and a composition of infinite skill."[5]

Robert S. Duncanson's *Land of the Lotus Eaters* remains one of the groundbreaking artist's most famous works. It led him to meet one of his literary heroes, but it may have had a racial subtext, too.

A year before Duncanson arrived, Tennyson entertained Giuseppe Garibaldi, the freedom fighter who led the effort to unify Italy's city-states. In September 1865, the poet welcomed none other than Queen Emma, monarch of the Hawaiian Islands. So, Robert Duncanson may have been a highly respected artist, but his visit to Tennyson's estate was overshadowed by the arrival of so many historic figures there during the same period.

While the date of Duncanson's trip to Tennyson's home is a mystery, one man did describe discussing the outing with the artist. Having recently relocated from Ohio to London, the Rev. Moncure D. Conway encountered Duncanson in the Kensington art gallery and made small talk with him. Duncanson revealed some remarkable news, and Conway wrote home about it. A Cincinnati newspaper printed part of his letter:

> He has been invited to come to London by various aristocratic personages. Among others, by the Duchess of Sutherland and the Duchess of Essex, who will be his patrons. He also received a letter from the poet laureate Tennyson; inviting him to visit … Think of a Negro sitting at the table with Mr. and Mrs. Alfred Tennyson, lord and lady of the manor, and mirror of Aristocracy, and so forth.[6]

The letter confirmed that Duncanson's career as an artist had truly exploded. He was not only famous but also sought after by some of the most distinguished people in the world. For an African American, the success Duncanson enjoyed was unprecedented.

Chapter 2

Artisan to Artist

Robert Duncanson's life and career can be summarized into a single word—"how." *How* did an African American, two generations removed from slavery, go from painting houses to painting portraits? And, from there, *how* did he become one of the premier landscape painters of the American Midwest?

Disputes About Duncanson

Robert S. Duncanson was born in or near the year of 1821. Detailed research conducted by art scholars James A. Porter[1] and Joseph D. Ketner[2] has led us to this conclusion, but the birthdate itself has long disappeared from the historical record. The limited information that exists about Duncanson's birth year comes from the 1860 US census and from Duncanson's passport application, filed in 1853.

Certainly, one can argue that it doesn't really matter if Duncanson was born in 1820, 1821, or 1822. What's most important is that Duncanson was a child of the early American republic. But his birthdate isn't the only aspect of his early life that's in dispute. His birthplace and

Could Duncanson Pass for White?

Surviving photographs of Robert S. Duncanson reveal him to be light-skinned with curly, rather than tightly coiled, hair. He clearly did not look like he was a man of solely African parentage, but could he pass for white, as friend Reuben Graham had accused him of doing?

A fifty-year-old Duncanson wrote to Graham to say, "You have stated that I have all my life tried to pass for white. Shame!! Shame!! Reuben. My heart has always been with the downtrodden race."[3]

Duncanson had, in fact, supported the abolitionist movement to end slavery. He spent time in largely white circles because white patrons supported his art, he explained. The artist added that the only color that mattered to him was paint color.

Even if Duncanson wanted to pass for white, could he have? The Rev. Moncure D. Conway, who met Duncanson in England in 1865, described him as a "Negro," and so did Franklin Blackwell Mayer, an artist who encountered him in Cincinnati in 1851.

ethnic identity have long remained in doubt, too. At one point, historians agreed—based on slim evidence—that Duncanson was the son of a free black woman and a Scots Canadian father. They also contended that Duncanson's middle initial, *S*, stood for Scott.

Years of careful research by Joseph D. Ketner have answered some of the lingering questions about Duncanson. He found that Duncanson was born in Fayette, New York, and that both of his parents were African American. Scholars probably assumed Duncanson was biracial because the few surviving photographs of the artist reveal that he was fairly light-skinned. But Duncanson did have a Scottish ancestor: his great-grandfather was a Virginia slaveholder whose family came from Scotland. Rather than a Scots Canadian father, Duncanson had a Scots American great-grandfather. And the middle initial *S* in Duncanson's name likely stood for Seldon, not Scott.

Early Life

Born circa 1745, Duncanson's grandfather was an enslaved black man named Charles Duncanson who gained his freedom after the Revolutionary War. Around the year 1790, he began his life as a free black person in Fayette, New York, thanks to a land grant to military veterans. This is where Robert S. Duncanson was born.

The Finger Lakes section of upstate New York was a decent place for a young African American in the 1820s. Blacks still experienced racism there, as there was no place a black person could escape bigotry in the United States. But the racial bias they faced wasn't virulent. The area also

This archival photo shows people rowing on Owasco Lake, in the Finger Lakes region of New York, in the late nineteenth century. It was taken by amateur photographer Charles Hadden.

offered black people more employment opportunities—at least in the manual trades.

At this time, the Finger Lakes region was in the final stages of a major religious revival. Part of the Second Great Awakening, this revival meant that the Duncansons and their neighbors heard many sermons, some of them presented outdoors. Duncanson seldom commented on religious matters as an adult, and chances are he was overexposed to fire-and-brimstone sermons in his youth.

We have virtually no records of Duncanson's early life—no diaries, letters, or keepsakes. The scant public records that do exist indicate that he grew up the second-

A Critical Difference

Artisans work in established trades and settings. They often create very fine products but do so in a standard or traditional manner. Artisans include a variety of occupations, such as watchmakers, furniture makers, shoemakers, and silversmiths. They typically begin as apprentices to learn their craft from workers who've long been in the field. Think of an apprenticeship like an internship–but for trades.

While artisans work in a very particular way, artists have more freedom to express themselves. They don't try to complete a painting in the same way that other artists would, for example. They strive to create something truly original. Artists may go to school to master their craft, but they may also be self-taught.

oldest son in a large family. Except for his eldest brother (who was mentally impaired), all the male Duncansons worked as carpenters, house painters, and glaziers (workers who handle glass for a living). Their grandfather specialized in all of these trades and passed them down to the younger Duncansons.

Robert's expertise in these fields would lead to his name appearing in an 1838 advertisement in a Monroe, Michigan, newspaper. The ad stated:

> John Gamblin and R. Duncanson, Painters and Glaziers, beg leave to acquaint their friends and the citizens of Monroe and its vicinity, that they have established themselves in the above business, and respectfully solicit patronage. They pledge themselves to do work in the most superior style, and to use the best and genuine materials.[4]

The Duncanson family had relocated to Monroe, on the western shore of Lake Erie, a few years earlier. Their solid record of workmanship made them financially better off than many African American families of the time. But Robert S. Duncanson's first venture into business lasted less than one year. The advertisement did not reappear, and by the 1840s, Duncanson left behind both Monroe and his family.

In 1841, Duncanson relocated to Cincinnati, Ohio. The Queen City, as many called it, had more than forty thousand people and was one of the busiest places in the American Midwest. Duncanson was one of thousands of people who moved to Cincinnati in the 1840s. Among them were many African Americans. But Duncanson differed from the city's other newcomers in that he was an *artisan* determined to become an *artist.*

It's unclear how Duncanson shifted from artisan to artist. He left no papers or artistic statements that shed light on this transition, so how he made the move is open to interpretation. Certainly, it helped that he already worked with paints and colors, and perhaps acquaintances,

This image from 1848 shows a steamboat on the Cincinnati, Ohio, waterfront.

either in Monroe or Cincinnati, assisted him. But it's also plausible that Duncanson began his career on his own. In other words, he was self-taught and simply used his will to succeed in an occupation that few found realistic for African Americans.

The oldest surviving Duncanson artwork dates to 1841. Measuring 30 by 25 inches (76 by 63.5 cm), *Portrait of a*

Mother and Daughter is currently in the possession of the Fulton County Arts Council of Atlanta. The painting may be speaking to the fragility of life. It features a very slim mother, about the age of thirty, and her cherubic child, about the age of ten. The daughter is wholesome and appealing, but the fine lines of the mother's face are more compelling. The parent is at the age when many Americans—black and white, rich and poor—succumbed to diphtheria, tuberculosis, and other infectious diseases. The child places an arm around her, begging the question: Who is protecting whom?

Art critics generally do not admire *Mother and Daughter*. The painting is too mannered, they say, meaning that it is very traditional. But this criticism, however justified from a technical standpoint, ignores that Duncanson had come this far on his own. *Mother and Daughter* marks the beginning of his start in the creative world. With the painting, he had achieved his goal of shifting from artisan to artist.

Chapter 3

An Artist's Growth

Robert S. Duncanson did not set out to make art that spoke to the social and economic conditions of his day. His work in these areas developed gradually—after the local community expressed interest in such themes. Since Duncanson was so talented that he could successfully approach a wide range of topics, he did not shy away from covering social commentary in his art.

Starting Out

A good deal is known about Cincinnati in the 1840s. Thanks to publications such as *Cincinnati in 1841*, we know that its population was roughly 45,000, including 2,200 African Americans. Cincinnati regarded itself as a city on the rise. As journalist Charles Cist wrote, "Cincinnati, the largest city of the west, is situated in a gradual bend of the Ohio River, on its northern bank, and immediately opposite Newport and Covington, Kentucky."[1] Cist went on to examine the commerce, banking, and agriculture in the city, as well as the rise of fine arts there. The Queen City had one daguerreotype (photographic) artist, four miniature painters, eight landscape and portrait painters, and four painters of ornaments and banners.[2] These are not small figures for a frontier city.

The publication did not include Duncanson in its list of artists. He had only just arrived, and it would take some time for him to make a name for himself. The ambitious painter was determined to join the ranks of Cincinnati's artistic community, but he did not move to the city right away. Rather, he lived in the village of Mount Healthy, about 15 miles (24 kilometers) north of Cincinnati. A variety of African American families, some of whom had ties to Duncanson's father and grandfather, helped him settle into the town.

The budding artist likely rented a room from the family of Reuben Graham in Mount Healthy. Before long, he met and married his wife, Rebecca. Duncanson never wrote anything about his first marriage, but a *Cincinnati Tribune* correspondent wrote an article in July 1846 that revealed some information about Duncanson's early art and wife. Abolitionist publication *The Liberator* reprinted the article, giving it a wider readership. It stated:

> I had a great treat last evening in the view of some portrait paintings and fancy pieces from the pencil of a *Negro.* He has been working as a common house painter and employed his leisure time in these works of art, and they are really beautiful; one fancy piece I was much struck with, a fruit and vegetable basket. The Negro was conveyed home to his family from market with a large basket filled with every variety of vegetables and fruit. As he reached home, the old wicker basket parted at one of the sides, and out tumbled the good provender. This suggested the idea of the picture.[3]

Duncanson finished many still-life paintings in the 1840s, but it's not clear which particular piece the writer describes. The article went on to provide details about Duncanson's wife. She had been enslaved in Nashville, which the writer knew because he had witnessed a "reunion" of sorts between Rebecca and a woman from the family who had kept her in bondage. Rebecca insisted that the woman accept two of her husband's paintings for free. The woman, however, said she did not think that would be right. She suggested Rebecca and Robert Duncanson should sell the pieces to her and put the money to good use. According to the writer, this comment led to an emotional response from Rebecca.

> The Negro burst into tears and said, "what do I care for $25? I would rather you should have the paintings then that I should receive $500," and she added that if her mistress did not take them, she would be forced to believe that she placed no value upon them. I turned from this scene between the mistress and the [former] slave and asked myself, wherein do the kindly feelings of gratitude which flow from the heart and throb in the bosom of the Negro differ from those of the white race?[4]

The writer was astonished that Rebecca could behave so kindly to a woman from the family who'd enslaved her. He wondered how an African American could show appreciation to whites in this way, while whites treated blacks with little regard.

The Drunkard's Plight (1845, oil on canvas) is part of the Detroit Institute of Arts' collection. It marked Duncanson's foray into using art for the purpose of social commentary.

Painting as Social Commentary

In 1845, Duncanson finished a powerful painting called *The Drunkard's Plight.* Completed in oil on canvas, *The Drunkard's Plight* shows an intoxicated man dressed in tattered clothing. He stands with his head turned, so the viewer can only make out half of his face. One presumes that he is hiding his "worse" half. A broken jug sits near his feet. Perhaps he broke it in a drunken stupor, or he threw it down in a fit of rage after being called out for his behavior. On the other hand, his wife or son might have cracked the jug open to prevent the man from drinking again.

The painting shows the drunkard's wife and young son making a possibly futile effort to reason with him. Another woman and child beckon to him from a dark doorway. They could be friends or other family members.

The Drunkard's Plight is a compelling painting because the viewer doesn't know what will become of the alcoholic man. Will he give up drinking and reform his ways, or will he return to the barroom, where he might have had a brawl? Duncanson leaves it up to the viewer to decide the drunkard's fate.

The Drunkard's Plight is not a masterpiece of composition. One can find fault in the lines and in the drunkard's wife,

Did Duncanson Have a Drinking Problem?

The Drunkard's Plight was one of the finest paintings Duncanson completed early in his career. The painting seems to be set in a Midwestern town, perhaps on one of the Great Lakes, and ships' sails beckon as a possible means of escape for the alcoholic man portrayed. Is there a piece of autobiography in this portrait?

Art historians do not believe Duncanson was an alcoholic. No firm evidence suggests that he drank heavily. But it is highly possible that the artist witnessed scenes like the one in *The Drunkard's Plight*. His friends, family members, or neighbors may have suffered from alcoholism, and he might have sympathized with them or their loved ones.

The painting hints that Duncanson might have identified with both the boy in the painting and with the alcoholic. On one hand, he wanted life to return to normal, as the boy did; on the other, he might have questioned, as the alcoholic likely did, if life could ever be normal under the cloud of addiction.

who is not especially convincing. She doesn't appear to be seriously troubled by the drunk man. In fact, the corners of her mouth are slightly upturned, as if she finds him humorous. That said, the painting is a great piece of social commentary. It shows a Midwestern family on the verge of breaking up because of alcohol's power over the husband. When Duncanson finished the painting, he was a married father who might have pondered the impact of alcoholism on families.

An Artist Matures

Duncanson made frequent trips to Detroit. Visiting the town meant that he probably observed ships transporting the first load of copper from the famous Cliff Mine on Michigan's northern peninsula. This would pay off for the artist, whose first major commission required him to paint the mine.

The commission, or job, came from the Rev. Charles Avery, a Pittsburgh abolitionist who owned Cliff Mine. Once hired, Duncanson worked steadily on the panting, which he completed in just a few months.

Held today in a private collection, *Cliff Mine, Lake Superior* measures 29 by 42 inches (74 by 107 cm). The mine may have been in Michigan, but Duncanson's use of copper hues gives the impression that it was located in the American West. Withered trees stand in the foreground of the painting, and a massive cliff fills up the background. Duncanson also painted the workers' cabins and a company store. The tiny human figures scattered throughout provide some warmth to what is otherwise a chilling scene of destruction.

The Temperance Movement

A generation before *The Drunkard's Plight* debuted, Americans were consuming far more hard liquor than people in a number of other countries did. But the temperance movement, led by middle-class white women, helped to curb this harmful habit. The movement led tens of thousands of men to sign temperance pledges, swearing to reduce their alcohol consumption.

When a person exercises temperance, one indulges in an activity (be it drinking or something else) in moderation. Temperance means to use restraint or self-control, and the temperance movement resulted in Americans cutting their alcohol consumption by roughly 50 percent.

The women of Madison, Minnesota, demonstrate for the prohibition of alcohol in their state, circa 1917. Women with alcoholic husbands were vulnerable to abuse, as were their children.

Cliff Mine, Lake Superior marked a great feat in Duncanson's development as an artist. It shows his growth from portraiture to thematic concepts and, finally, landscape painting. It's not known how Avery reacted to the painting, but he must have liked it well enough, as he and the artist

This is a general vew of the Cliff Shaft Mine Head Frame in Ishpeming, Marquette County, Michigan.

continued to have a relationship. In fact, Duncanson would later loan him a painting.

By the late 1840s, Duncanson had established himself as an up-and-coming painter in Cincinnati. Local critics helped his reputation by giving his work positive reviews. During this time, he also experimented with daguerreotypes, an early form of photographs.

Duncanson's decision to move to Cincinnati had worked out well for him. The Queen City (the name came from a steamboat) prided itself on being the most advanced place in the American Midwest. By the early 1850s, Cincinnati had nearly one hundred residents who identified themselves as "artists" in the census. The city was moving forward, but some believed it still had progress to make.

The Midwest lagged behind the East Coast because it had been developed later than New York and Philadelphia. Older cities were already home to an artistic tradition. Money also played a role in the success of eastern cities. Cincinnati could not hope to compete with New York in terms of wealth, but the city was gradually attracting rich men who had the ability to be patrons of the fine arts.

Chapter 4

Friends and Patrons

By the late 1840s, Robert Duncanson was known throughout Cincinnati's African American community. He was also acquainted with the city's group of abolitionists, the men and women who worked to end slavery. But he needed more friends and benefactors. His art had progressed to a strong level, but he couldn't continue painting without financial backers.

Detroit and Cincinnati

Duncanson's permanent residence was in Cincinnati, but he made frequent, and sometimes lengthy, trips to Detroit. Perhaps the Queen City contained too much competition; then again, Duncanson may have found Detroit's habitat more inspiring than Cincinnati's landscape. In any case, his reputation as a great artist was growing. One Detroit publication described Duncanson as follows:

> Mr. Duncanson has already taken the portraits of a number of our citizens and has designed and finished several historical and fancy pieces of great merit. The portraits are very accurate likenesses and executed

This photo of Detroit City Hall was taken circa 1900. Detroit would play an inportant role in Robert S. Duncanson's life and career.

> with great skill and lifelike coloring … Mr. Duncanson deserves, and we trust will receive the patronage of all lovers of the fine arts.[1]

Duncanson sold a number of paintings in Detroit. His next commission, however, came from a Cincinnati businessman. It was one of the most important jobs of his budding art career, and it came from Ohio's richest man, Nicholas Longworth.

As a young man, Longworth had moved from New Jersey to Cincinnati. He began as a lawyer but quickly mastered the art of buying real estate. He already owned a great deal of valuable land, but a set of wineries he'd started in the 1820s and 1830s significantly increased his wealth. His "Catawba" wines were the most popular in the Midwest.

The businessman had more than a passing interest in art. According to some reports, he met his wife at an art gallery and, perhaps out of gratitude, became Cincinnati's top art patron. He even "discovered" Hiram Powers, the Vermont-born sculptor who moved to Cincinnati as a teenager, to Washington in his thirties, and to Italy after that.

Hiram Powers was an inspiration to Robert Duncanson. Duncanson realized that without the patronage of Nicholas Longworth, the sculptor would not have enjoyed so much success. Given this, Duncanson was thrilled when Longworth commissioned him to paint murals directly on plaster walls in Belmont, the businessman's Cincinnati home. Duncanson received this incredible opportunity in either 1848 or early 1849.

This is an engraved portrait of Nicholas Longworth, who cultivated strawberries and grapes and became one of the nation's first winemakers.

Belmont was no ordinary house. Located on the outskirts of the city, Longworth's home was large enough to house all the people with that name, or so he claimed. Belmont was more of a mansion than a house, but it lacked the touches of elegance that could make it really stand out. Art could help distinguish the mansion from the other large homes in Cincinnati.

Hiram Powers

Born in 1805 in Vermont, Hiram Powers had an early life that very much resembled Duncanson's. (The main difference between the two was that Powers was white.) Both artists moved from the East Coast to the Midwest. Powers made the move as a teenager, settling in Ohio, where Nicholas Longworth became his patron. A patron is someone who donates money to certain causes, especially art-related ones. Patrons give money to artists to allow them to devote time to their craft without having to work to support themselves. Musicians, fine artists, poets, and writers are some of the professionals who have traditionally received help from patrons.

Having established himself as an artist due to Longworth's patronage, Powers relocated to Washington, DC. But before he left, he sculpted a worthy bust of Longworth. After living in the nation's capital, Powers headed to Italy, which had a large community of American sculptors.

He and Longworth stayed in touch by writing letters to each other. Powers died in 1873.

This is an engraved portrait of sculptor Hiram Powers, one of the most influential sculptors to come out of the United States. He later became a member of the expatriate artist community in Italy.

Duncanson eagerly accepted Longworth's offer. He was not one to back down from a challenge. And the task Longworth had given him had the potential to change the artist's life.

Duncanson needed more than a year to complete the eight landscape murals and the smaller ornaments and decorations that accompanied them. Sadly, there is no newspaper account of his creative process, and Longworth's descendants covered up the murals in the passing years. For almost five decades, the murals lay undetected beneath sheets of fancy wallpaper. But when that paper was removed, around the year 1930, viewers were treated to something truly exceptional—the largest set of landscape murals completed before the Civil War.

Entering the house today, which has since been converted to the Taft Museum of Art, the viewer first sees Duncanson's foyer murals. These are relatively quiet and tame, and they evoke European landscapes the artist hadn't encountered before painting them. Without having seen them, how did Duncan summon up these pastoral scenes? The most logical answer is that he read a good deal of English poetry, and the descriptions in the writing helped him imagine what the landscapes looked like.

Duncanson's murals for Longworth include a number of scenes that portray both the European and American countryside. Today, these scenes can be found in the main section of the Taft Museum.

In Duncanson's murals, the human figures are consistently small, sometimes even tiny. Though the artist never called himself a Hudson River School painter, he was influenced by the school's methods. He embraced the

The Taft Museum

The Longworth home became the Taft Museum in the 1930s. Today, it remains one of the finest examples of elegant Midwestern architecture. Duncanson's murals remain a major draw to tourists and art specialists alike. The Taft Museum also endows a special fund to support the Robert S. Duncanson Artist-in-Residence Program. Though Duncanson never lived within its walls, the museum is perhaps the place where his memory is most honored.

The Taft Museum of Art is in Cincinnati, Ohio. Built circa 1820 for merchant Martin Baum, it was later the home of Nicholas Longworth.

idea that nature is grand and humans are puny. Nature will be here forever, but humans are small, transient creatures on the landscape. Again, Duncanson must have been remarkably talented to have pulled these scenes off with no formal artistic training.

He completed the Belmont murals by 1850 and established a lasting friendship with Nicholas Longworth during the process. The businessman introduced him to a number of other powerful people in the Cincinnati community. While he continued to need patrons, Duncanson was also ready to complete some paintings that had not been commissioned. He wanted to fulfil his own artistic vision.

Blue Hole

In 1851, Duncanson completed one of his best-known paintings, *Blue Hole, Flood Waters, Little Miami River*. Completed in oil on canvas and measuring 22 by 28 inches (56 by 71 cm), *Blue Hole* depicts a well-known place on the Little Miami River. The spot is flooded because of rising waters on the main branch of the river. *Blue Hole* depicts nature as a splendid ruin. Enormous tree trunks seem to vanish in the murky water, and the granite boulders on the far side of the hole look as if they are meant to build a new set of pyramids.

Three human figures can be seen near the water. A young man, perhaps in his late teens, has his back to the viewer, as he's focused on fishing. A friend handles a fishing rod but seems confused, so a third person assists. This individual is dressed in army green. A large hat obscures his face, but it's evident that this older man will guide the younger ones.

Art historians regard *Blue Hole* as a masterpiece. The artist managed to capture dozens of trees and even found enough space to depict individual leaves. The overall scene displays nature's potency as well as the fleeting quality of all creation. The floods of spring allow for the bounty of summer, which gives way to autumn. This characteristic of the painting is perhaps why *Blue Hole* is one of Duncanson's most admired works.

Chapter 5

Hudson River School

The Hudson River School was not a traditional school with classrooms and teachers. It was an informal group of American painters who believed that nature was more important than humanity. While that idea seemingly clashes with Christianity, many people of all denominations believed in both the scriptures and the significance of nature. As a painter of landscapes, Duncanson's work can be categorized within that artistic movement.

Inspired by Cincinnati

Sometime in 1851, Duncanson finished *View of Cincinnati, Ohio, from Covington, Kentucky*. Measuring 25 by 36 inches (63.5 by 91 cm), *View of Cincinnati* is based on a daguerreotype made three years earlier. Art historians can line up the daguerreotype and the painting and identify the small but important differences.

Duncanson's painting features a broad sky, three major trees, and a landscape separated into the Ohio and

Robert Duncanson finished his painting *View of Cincinnati, Ohio, from Covington, Kentucky* in 1851. It reveals how the Hudson River School influenced him.

Kentucky sides of the Ohio River. Three figures—two white children and a black man with a scythe—appear in the middle of the foreground. One can almost hear a conversation in which the children pose questions to the man and he answers them. To the right of the trio sits a house and barn. A black woman, presumably the wife of the man, is hanging laundry on a clothesline.

Some observers have argued that the man is in a subservient position, but the scene does not bear this

Cincinnati's Unique Location

Throughout the 1850s, Cincinnati was a flash point for racial, ethnic, and economic tension. Race riots had taken place in each of the three previous decades. Although a majority of Cincinnatians favored the gradual abolition of slavery, plenty of their friends and relatives on both sides of the river disagreed with this idea. While some of these residents wanted slavery to continue, others wanted slavery to end quickly, not gradually.

Cincinnati was also home to the Stowes, a famous family of abolitionists. In 1836, Calvin Ellis Stowe married Harriet Beecher, who would author the famous novel *Uncle Tom's Cabin* based on the stories she heard from African Americans who'd escaped slavery. Both she and her husband were fierce critics of the institution.

Harriet Beecher Stowe was an American novelist, most famous for writing the antislavery book *Uncle Tom's Cabin*. She poses with her hand on her chin.

out. Rather, his body language shows that he is in a position of strength and dignity. His wife is harder to make out, but their dwelling is no crude cabin. This couple lives rather well.

Finally, there, in the background, is the city of Cincinnati. Unlike the Kentucky side of the river, Cincinnati is portrayed as a shimmering vision of the urban world. Smoke rises from at least twenty locations, be they house chimneys or factories. The overall impression is a mixture of urban and rural, North and South.

Uncle Tom and Little Eva

Just one year after Robert Duncanson completed *View of Cincinnati*, the Queen City had become more famous than ever. Harriet Beecher Stowe had raised the city's profile, despite relocating to Maine after nearly twenty years in Cincinnati. A Boston publisher released

Robert S. Duncanson's painting *Uncle Tom and Little Eva* (1853, oil on canvas) was unfortunately considered to be an artistic flop by critics.

her groundbreaking novel *Uncle Tom's Cabin; or, Life Among the Lowly*.

To label *Uncle Tom's Cabin* a best seller would be an understatement. It was the best-selling book of the entire nineteenth century, and it changed many people's minds about slavery. Many Northerners who had previously been on the fence about slavery condemned it after reading the gripping novel.

In the wake of the book's success, a Detroit minister commissioned Duncanson to complete a painting on the subject. Though the commission came at the right time, it was one of Duncanson's few disasters. The artist generally enjoyed good press, but critics almost universally regarded Duncanson's *Uncle Tom and Little Eva* as a flop, if not an outright disaster.

Done in oil on canvas and measuring 28 by 39 inches (71 by 99 cm), *Uncle Tom and Little Eva* today belongs to the Detroit Institute of Arts. The scene is taken directly from Harriet Beecher Stowe's novel. Duncanson places the character of Eva almost dead center. Clad in white, with a touch of red around the waist, she points to the sky to signal that it is her time to go to God.

The background is a mixture of rich green plants and a dull waterscape. Seated on a rock or log, Uncle Tom holds Little Eva's left hand with his right. His face is angled so the viewer can see just half of his countenance. Plus, Duncanson makes Uncle Tom so dark that it is hard to read his expression.

The most scathing review of *Uncle Tom and Little Eva* came from the pages of the *Cincinnati Commercial Gazette*. A critic wrote:

> An Uncle Tomitude.—Uncle Tom, according to the artist, is a very stupid looking creature, and Eva, instead of being a fragile and fading flower, is a rosy-complexioned, healthy-seeming girl, not a bit ethereal. She is complacently pointing toward a portion of the canvas which is deeply yellow, with a dusky-red fringe—probably intended to be a sunset. Tom has nearly all of her arm in his hand, as if intending

Death of His Spouse

When Rebecca Duncanson died is unknown. But chances are, it happened prior to 1853, the year Robert Duncanson painted *Uncle Tom and Little Eva*.

The artist and his late wife had two children during their marriage, and he might have felt ill-equipped to become a single father. His wife's death might have left him so distraught that it affected his art. It could have contributed to his underwhelming painting *Uncle Tom and Little Eva*. The grief process can be lengthy, and the widower likely needed more time to recover from his loss before diving back into his work. That said, some people find that losing themselves in their art helps them cope with their grief.

At some point, Duncanson married his second wife, Phoebe. Little is known about her, except that she was biracial and had a son with the artist. His name was Mittie.[1]

> to check the projected flight, and appears about to inquire—what goin' dar for?[2]

The reviews were almost unanimous: *Uncle Tom and Little Eva* was an utter failure. Even for the modern viewer, Duncanson's depiction of Uncle Tom as a stupid hulking brute is hard to digest. How could the artist have flopped so badly? How could he handle landscapes and individual portraits so well but perform miserably when depicting a fellow African American? Duncanson may have been at odds with his ethnicity. Being light-skinned was an advantage to him throughout his life, and he was truly insensitive when depicting a dark-skinned black man on canvas.

Trip Abroad

Given his sensitive and intense nature, Duncanson was very likely disturbed by the reviews of *Uncle Tom and Little Eva*. Fortunately, he was able to shake the dust of Cincinnati from his feet.

Whether it was a sudden decision or long in the planning is unknown, but Duncanson left for Europe in March 1853. Precisely where he secured the funds for the trip is uncertain. Nicholas Longworth might have helped pay for his trip abroad. Then again, Longworth might have directed Duncanson to other abolitionists for help. In any case, Duncanson was able to make the trip, along with the artist William Louis Sonntag.

Sonntag and Duncanson were both landscape painters, and they had worked in adjoining studios for several years.

It was logical for them to travel together. Armed with letters of introduction, they set out in 1853.

Duncanson carried a letter from Nicholas Longworth to Hiram Powers. Nearly twenty years had passed since Powers left Cincinnati for Washington, DC, and then Florence, Italy. Longworth penned strong words of support for Duncanson, describing him as a person and artist of great merit. Sonntag was the more experienced artist, Longworth declared, but the businessman added that he believed that Duncanson would eventually become the more well-known of the two.

Chapter 6

Becoming a Master

Duncanson's trip to Europe in 1853 was a major turning point in his life and career. Like most American artists, Duncanson had turned to western Europe for inspiration. Even though he was already a first-rate painter of the American countryside, Duncanson admired the works of European artists and believed he could benefit from seeing their works up close.

Painting a Masterpiece

Duncanson is said to have been the first African American artist to make the so-called Grand Tour of western Europe. Duncanson and Sonntag initially arrived in England, where they toured London and sections of the countryside. The rural scenes delighted Duncanson, but he said little about London's noise and congestion, which worsened each year.

Departing England, Duncanson and Sonntag crossed the English Channel, the body of water between southern England and northern France. After France, they made their way to Switzerland and northern Italy. Arriving in

Florence, they spent several months with the American artistic community there and probably spoke at length with Hiram Powers, then the most successful of the American expatriate artists.

Duncanson and Sonntag both returned to the United States in early 1854. Sonntag soon moved to New York City, where he achieved major success as a landscape painter, but Duncanson did not have any sense of inferiority as a result. In a revealing letter to the self-taught white artist Junius Sloan, Duncanson declared:

> Every day that breaks to my vision, sheds new light over my path. What was once dark and misty is gradually becoming brighter. My trip to Europe has to some extent enabled me to judge of my own talent. Of all the landscapes I saw in Europe (and I saw thousands) I did not feel discouraged.[1]

Duncanson suggested in the letter that the group of American artists he met in Europe weren't doing anything very exciting in landscape painting. Though he did not specifically name Sonntag, he might have very well lumped him in with this unoriginal set of painters. Duncanson, on the other hand, was accomplishing something new.

By the late 1850s, Duncanson was known throughout the Midwest. Much of his audience realized he was black, but some of his admirers were completely unaware of the fact. Duncanson preferred not to discuss race because he was most interested in making work that would be remembered for decades. Most American painters at this time strived to create a masterpiece, and Duncanson

William Louis Sonntag's landscape painting *Dream of Italy* is in the Dayton Art Institute in Dayton, Ohio.

worked on his, *Land of the Lotus Eaters*, for roughly six months before its unveiling in May 1861.

By then, the Civil War had started with the Battle of Fort Sumter in Charleston, South Carolina. The election of Abraham Lincoln to the presidency in November 1860 had practically guaranteed the South would secede from, or leave, the Union. Seven states left during the winter of 1860–1861, and four others followed after the Battle of Fort Sumter on April 12, 1861.

Land of the Lotus Eaters debuted as the Union crumbled, but this fact didn't result in the painting, widely considered a masterpiece, being overlooked. The *Cincinnati Gazette* praised the painting as follows:

Robert H. Duncanson, Esquire has just completed and places on exhibition his painting, the Lotus Eaters, from Tennyson's poem of that name. Mr. Duncanson has long enjoyed the enviable reputation of being the best landscape painter in the West, and his latest effort cannot fail to raise him still higher in

The Timing of *Lotus Eaters*

Was it just a coincidence that Duncanson unveiled *Land of the Lotus Eaters* shortly after the Civil War began? Duncanson rarely commented on the timing of his art, but he probably started the painting in December 1860, the same month that South Carolina left the Union. The secession of that state signaled that other states would follow and a full-on war would break out between the North and the South.

Art historian Joseph D. Ketner did not believe that the timing of *Lotus Eaters* was simply due to chance. He argued that the conflict between the North and the South influenced Duncanson to start the painting. Ketner contends that the natives of the lotus land represent African Americans, and the lotus plants symbolize the South's addiction to slavery. Duncanson considered the institution to be a tragedy for both the enslaved and the slaveholder.

This illustration depicts the attack on Fort Sumter, April 12 and 13, 1861, which kicked off the Civil War.

R.S.D.
1862.

Robert S. Duncanson's *Maiden's Rock, Lake Pepin* (1862, oil on canvas) is a stunning painting that shows the artist's immense skill and mastery of the landscape.

> the estimation of the art loving public. He has not only wooed but won his favorite muse. [2]

Other publications applauded the painting as well, leading Duncanson to exhibit the piece for much longer than he'd anticipated. Close friends also knew he intended to take *Lotus Eaters* to England to show the Brits just what an American artist could accomplish.

Additional Landscapes

The grandchild of an enslaved man, Duncanson's opposition to slavery certainly seems sincere, but he was not an active abolitionist, nor did he play a role in the Civil War. He was an artist first and foremost, and he prioritized his work above all else. During late 1861 and early 1862, Duncanson was frequently on the road, where he sketched landscape scenes he later turned into full-sized paintings. Two of the numerous scenes he painted are especially attention-worthy.

Completed in 1862 in oil on canvas, *The Falls of Minnehaha* is now held in a private collection. It is nearly a perfect depiction of the natural world, as it features hundreds of water drops cascading. The end result is a sublime painting that can hold the viewer's attention for hours, thanks to Duncanson's marvelous ability to capture a moment in time in captivating fashion.

The artist's 1862 painting *Maiden's Rock, Lake Pepin* is not as well known as *The Falls of Minnehaha*, but it is just as powerful. Today, the oil on canvas work is part of the permanent collection of the Meade Art Museum at Amherst College. The painting shows the light of early

How Long?

How long does it take to become a great artist? The time involved varies, as some artists have a knack for the work that might allow them to progress more rapidly than others. Self-taught, Duncanson clearly possessed a great deal of natural talent, but he excelled in his profession at a fairly average rate.

He spent his 1840s as a traveling artist, painting what he could in bits and pieces. The following decade, he gained a high level of competence, and by the 1860s, he began to create masterpieces.

morning bathing the rocky cliffs on the water's edge. A small sailboat with three figures inside appears in the center-right portion of the piece. The figures look tiny compared to their surroundings, which falls in line with the Hudson River School philosophy about the relationship between nature and humanity.

The landscape paintings Duncanson finished after his masterpiece *Land of the Lotus Eaters* show how he continued to evolve as an artist. *The Falls of Minnehaha* and *Maiden's Rock* suggest that he wasn't content with the success and international acclaim he'd achieved. He was devoted to his art and would keep exploring new themes and landscapes well after he'd matured as a painter.

Chapter 7

International Acclaim

As the Civil War continued to rage, Duncanson made up his mind to focus on his art. Sometime in 1862, the same year he sketched and painted in the upper Midwest, Duncanson made a short tour of northern New England. He painted several New Hampshire scenes before crossing the border into British Canada.

Fame in Canada

The US-Canadian border was a familiar area for Duncanson since he'd grown up in upstate New York and spent his formative years on the western end of Lake Erie. To cross over and live as a Canadian, however, was something quite different. It was an important move for him to make for his development as an artist, and it allowed him to escape from the Civil War. A number of Americans, black or white, did not have this option.

Within a few short months of living in Canada, Duncanson's fame grew widely. He enjoyed even more success in Canada than he had in America. The Canadians did not place as much emphasis on Duncanson's ethnicity as Americans had. They were simply pleased that an important American had come to their country to paint Canadian landscapes.

During his time in Canada, Duncanson formed a partnership with Canada's leading photographer, William Notman. The two worked as a team, with Notman doing most of the photography and Duncanson painting the images taken. Their most successful collaborations included *City and Harbor of Quebec* (1863), *On the St. Anne's, East Canada* (1863–1865), and *River with Rapids* (1864).

Painting Canadian landscapes was a challenge for Duncanson because he was used to his native Midwest. His best Canadian work involved water scenes, such as *Canadian Falls* (1865) and *Sunset Study* (1863). While it took time for him to adapt to the Canadian setting, the people there continued to revere him. He felt more appreciated in Toronto and Montreal than he ever had in Cincinnati. Even today, Duncanson is better known in Canada than he is in the United States.

Crossing the Ocean

Photographs of Duncanson's art had reached England as early as 1864, and the enthusiastic response led him to plan a major trip abroad. In 1865, he sailed for Ireland, intending to display *Lotus Eaters* and *Western Forest* at the Dublin International Art Show. The *Illustrated London Times* featured pictures of the Dublin exhibit, and one newspaper illustration even shows workers carrying Duncanson's paintings off the ship and into the staging areas.

Duncanson was well received in Dublin, but not wildly so. In London, however, he was a star. The *Art Journal* wrote the following about *Lotus Eaters*:

Artist Winslow Homer completed his Civil War painting *Prisoners from the Front* in 1866. By moving to Canada, Duncanson was able to escape the politics of the Civil War that dominated American life.

William Notman (shown here) and Robert S. Duncanson collaborated together, taking hundreds of photos during the process. A few of these photos revealed what Duncanson looked like.

> The picture is full of fancy. It is a grand conception and a composition of infinite skill; yet every portion of it has been studied with the severest care, from "the charming sunset lingering adown in the red West" to the "slender streams," "some like a downward smoke," that bear the contributions of the mountains to the valley. The picture is of large size and has obviously been a work of time but time well bestowed. The sight of it cannot fail to be a source of intense enjoyment.[1]

Photographs of Duncanson

Duncanson and Notman took hundreds of photographs, but just a few reveal what the landscape painter looked like. One shows him wearing the traditional beaver fur hat of the Canadian farmers. Two others capture him in a studio setting, and one of this pair very much frames him as a serious artist.

In the photograph, Duncanson wears a deep side part in his hair and slicked-down curls. He has a full mustache, furrowed brows, and faint lines in the center of his forehead. He appears to be in deep thought–and very likely was. The artist is presented as a dignified and respectable man.

Similar praise of the *Lotus Eaters* could be found in other journals, too. Visiting England when the United States was very much in the news had been a savvy decision by Duncanson. The American Civil War ended in April 1865, and Duncanson arranged for his works to be shown abroad just weeks afterward. The artist had even won an invite to meet the esteemed poet Alfred, Lord Tennyson at his country estate on the Isle of Wight. Very few other Americans could say the same.

After his success in Dublin and London, Duncanson could have treated Glasgow as an afterthought, but he

Did Favoritism Give Duncanson a Boost?

Robert S. Duncanson had proven himself to be a top-notch artist by the 1860s, but his talent might not have been solely responsible for the warm reception he received in countries such as Canada and England. Favoritism might have also played a role.

Duncanson had one very influential admirer–Harriet Howard, the Duchess of Sutherland. The duchess was said to be familiar with Duncanson's work years before he arrived in England in the 1860s. Charlotte Cushman, an American actress who spent time in Cincinnati, had described Duncanson's art to her. And it is possible that even Queen Victoria was familiar with Duncanson's pieces.

Harriet Howard admired Duncanson and may have played a role in getting influential people in Canada and Great Britain to support his work. This portrait of her was painted by Franz Xaver Winterhalter.

admired all things Scottish. Very likely, this is the reason several biographers mistakenly believed his middle initial stood for Scott.

As he toured Scotland, Duncanson fell in love with its countryside. He finished many sketches, some of which he later turned into full-size paintings. He had found the inspiration for what would be his final round of paintings. By the time he returned to the United States, Duncanson could truthfully make the claim that he was the first African American artist to break through to an international audience.

In Europe, Duncanson had also benefited from the amount of attention Great Britain paid to the antislavery cause. England had abolished its own slave trade decades before the United States had, and Queen Victoria was particularly interested in seeing the slave trade disappear. The English had also taken an interest in the Civil War because so many industrial workers in Britain had lost their jobs during the conflict, which had resulted in a production slowdown.

Chapter 8

Highland Overtones

By mid-1866, Duncanson was back at work in Cincinnati. Many of his friends and patrons had no idea what a welcome Great Britain had given him, but they did notice that Duncanson was more interested in painting Scottish landscapes than American ones. Clearly, his time abroad had greatly influenced his art.

New Work

Now in the Cincinnati Art Museum, 1867's *Rising Mist* is a Duncanson painting that was almost certainly inspired by the artist's travels abroad. The painting features a scene that Duncanson probably saw in Scotland or England's Lake Country. It shows a dark green hillside scattered with rocks, shrubs, and sheep. At the foot of the hillside is a small lake with a sailboat and rowboat of some sort. Tiny figures sit in the boats and stand next to them. Another figure, likely the shepherd, can be found with his dog beneath a tree on the hillside. It is the one tree in the painting, but Duncanson uses it masterfully to create an image of shadow. Low-hanging clouds cover the mountains in the background as mist rises from the lake.

Could Duncanson have found his inspiration for *Rising Mist* somewhere in the United States or Canada? That's unlikely, as the scene points to the Scottish countryside. The painting marked another success for the artist, who took a risk and advanced in his career yet again.

The same year *Rising Mist* debuted, Duncanson unveiled *Loch Long, Scotland*. Now part of the Smithsonian Institution collection, *Loch Long* is more refined than *Rising Mist*, but it is not as recognizably Scottish. If not for the painting's title, the viewer could mistake the setting for upstate New York. In this piece, the human figures are again very small to show how secondary they are to nature.

Why Scotland?

Why Scotland and not Wales? Why the Highlands and not Ireland? The answer lies in the main themes of British literature from the mid-nineteenth century. Given that Duncanson was a fan of literature, he very likely knew the novels of Sir Walter Scott. They were extremely popular during this time.

Duncanson's ability to paint such a variety of landscapes–the American Midwest, Canada, and then Scotland–shows that he was at the top of his game in the late 1860s. One wonders what he would have painted had he received the opportunity to travel to other parts of the world, such as Africa, Asia, or Latin America.

The year 1867 was a productive one for Duncanson, who also turned out *Pass at Leny*, his largest composition of a European scene to date. Measuring 18 by 30 inches (46 by 76 cm), *Pass at Leny* is owned by the Procter and Gamble Company of Cincinnati. In this work, Duncanson attempts to depict the Scottish wilderness and the daring travelers who passed through it. Perhaps on their way to the Scottish Highlands, two horsemen pass through a clearing of mountains and trees. Observing their movement, a lonely figure stands perhaps 50 yards (45 meters) behind them. Does he wish to join them, or does he believe they are making a potentially deadly journey? Viewers must interpret the scene for themselves.

Three years would pass before Duncanson painted his best Scottish works. Done in oil on canvas, the 1870 painting *Dog's Head of Scotland* now belongs to Boston's Museum of Fine Arts. The painting is based on some part of the Scottish coast, but Duncanson may have added details from his imagination, making it almost impossible to identify the precise place.

In the piece, Duncanson uses shades of gray to create a scene that looks like it's in the late afternoon. Clouds above suggest that an enormous storm has come and gone, and several men haul in the ruins of a fishing boat as two steamships sit in the distance. The painting implies that nature dictates all, but humans respond the best way they can to it. They are at its mercy.

The following year, Duncanson completed *Ellen's Isle, Loch Katrine*, a painting that's now in the Detroit Museum of Art. This piece is considered one of the artist's finest works.

The setting sun casts just enough light to allow the viewer to see Ellen's Isle in the middle of the lake (or loch). The island is thickly wooded and looks mysterious, perhaps even magical. Duncanson intended to give the painting to abolitionist Charles Sumner, a US senator. This context

Robert S. Duncanson's 1867 painting *Rising Mist* is in the Cincinnati Art Museum in Ohio.

highlights the importance of the canoes in *Ellen's Isle*, as the people inside may be African Americans fleeing slavery.

Nearing the End

In 1871, Duncanson was only about fifty years old, but

he seemed to sense that his time was running out. He wanted to make the most of every week and season and devoted himself to creating a new masterpiece. *Sunset on the New England Coast* represents a major artistic departure for the artist. While Duncanson had painted Scottish island and coastal scenes, this painting marked his first time capturing an American coastal scene.

Now in the Cincinnati Art Museum, *Sunset* is a powerful but disturbing work. It shows a massive rocky headland, with waves crashing from the east. One suspects that the coast of Maine was the model for this scene. The waves are large enough to overtake any human, but the clouds also look threatening.

Robert S. Duncanson completed this serene landscape painting, *Ellen's Isle, Loch Katrine*, in 1867.

Sunset on the New England Coast was a stunning painting, but Duncanson completed it during a time when his mental state was deteriorating.

Scholars now believe that Duncanson was suffering from dementia at the start of the 1870s, and he may have shown signs earlier as well. Family and friends had already noticed some bizarre behavior from him in private, but before long, his strange episodes became public knowledge.

The stress of being an African American artist in a white man's world certainly placed pressure on his fragile mind, but Duncanson also faced an unseen threat—his art. He likely suffered from a form of dementia brought on by long-term contact with paints and oils. Scholar Joseph

The Rejected Painting

At some point in 1871, Robert S. Duncanson traveled to Boston, where he tried to present *Ellen's Isle, Loch Katrine* to Senator Charles Sumner, but the politician declined the present. He explained that he made a point of never accepting gifts while in office. This was to show that he couldn't be bought, that no one could sway his political actions with a reward or bribe.

Duncanson, though, didn't seem to understand Sumner's moral code. The artist was deeply hurt that the politician had refused his gift of the painting. He took it personally, but Sumner's decision to turn away *Ellen's Isle* had nothing to do with the quality of the work or with Duncanson as a human being.

D. Ketner explained that Duncanson would have been exposed to lead paint during his house-painting days.

Lead paint has a toxic effect that would have accumulated as Duncanson continued to mash his colors and prepare them for his canvases.[1] At this time, Duncanson had completed dozens of works of art, and who knows how many houses he'd painted? Altogether, he'd been exposed to a large amount of lead, and it had taken a toll on his health—and his career.

Chapter 9

Sad Demise

Having achieved international success, Robert S. Duncanson reached the age of fifty, but he was already in the throes of a mysterious illness that would eventually kill him. As early as 1870, Duncanson displayed signs of hyperactivity and elation, with corresponding depression. Given that he had always been high-strung, friends and family did not worry much. Then, the symptoms worsened, and Duncanson had a seizure and collapsed in 1872. He had been hanging his paintings for an exhibit in Detroit.

Duncanson's Death

After his collapse, Duncanson behaved erratically and showed signs of schizophrenia. At one point, he thought a great woman painter had taken over his body to help him create masterpieces. As a result of such delusions, he was committed to a mental institution called the Detroit Retreat. Just three months later, he was dead.

The local newspapers were full of praise for Duncanson. The obituaries mentioned his many accomplishments. For example, the *Detroit Tribune* stated:

> Robert S. Duncanson, a celebrated artist of this country, died at the Michigan State Retreat on Michigan Avenue … He came to this city about three months since, and has been a patient in the above institution most of the time since. He had acquired the idea that in all his artistic efforts he was aided by the spirit of one of the great masters, and this so worked upon his mind as to affect him not only mentally but physically. He was 55 years of age, a man of modest and retiring disposition, and a gentleman who was greatly esteemed by all who knew him.[1]

The single most moving testimony came from the pages of the *Cincinnati Enquirer*. The paper described Duncanson as a devoted husband and father who had paid tribute to the Queen City both at home and abroad. The *Enquirer* also pointed out how successful he'd been as an artist. Yet, Duncanson was always willing to answer questions from aspiring artists who sought his advice, according to the paper. In conclusion, the *Enquirer* expressed the hope that the painter was walking among one of the heavenly landscapes he'd captured on canvas.[2]

Forgotten Artist

Robert S. Duncanson was widely praised after his death, but in the passing years, his contributions to art were forgotten. This fate befalls many painters after their deaths, but it is especially tragic that Duncanson's achievements were overlooked since he was such a trailblazer. The generations of African Americans who followed were deprived of the chance to celebrate his work.

Black art historian James A. Porter played a key role in renewing public interest in Duncanson's legacy. His lengthy 1951 article in *Art in America* clarified numerous misconceptions about Duncanson. Later, scholar Joseph D. Ketner would examine Duncanson's life and art as well. The misinformation about Duncanson included that he was a biracial black man educated in Canada instead of

The (Newspaper's) Last Word

Although the newspapers had praised Robert S. Duncanson's many contributions to the art world, most did not mention that he was African American. Readers who saw the artist's obituary learned that he was a complex and talented painter, but they learned nothing about his racial background.

The obituary writers might have believed that they were doing Duncanson a favor by ignoring his race. They might have assumed that white readers would not have taken an interest in his life and death had they known he was a person of color. But African American readers may have appreciated knowing that one of the Midwest's most accomplished painters had been a black man. That said, race was rarely the focus of Duncanson's art, so the press might have viewed him as an artist who happened to be black and not as a black artist.

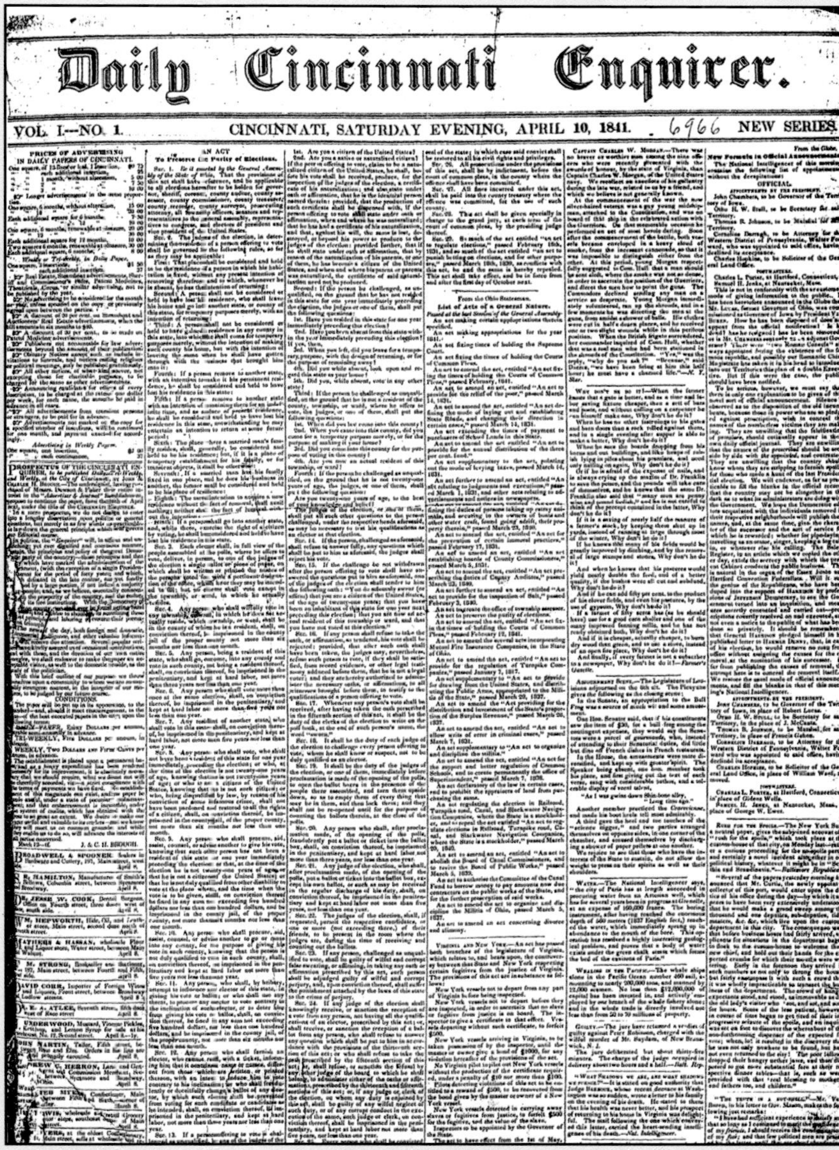

Daily Cincinnati Enquirer.

VOL. I.—NO. 1. CINCINNATI, SATURDAY EVENING, APRIL 10, 1841. 6966 NEW SERIES.

This image shows the April 10, 1841, edition of the *Cincinnati Enquirer*. The newspaper published a moving obituary for Duncanson after his death in 1872.

the New York–born son of two black parents with mixed racial ancestry.

Perhaps Duncanson's racial ancestry was misunderstood for so long because he didn't emphasize his ethnic background while alive. In Cincinnati, he moved between the white and black communities to a greater degree than most African Americans. This was due to the lightness of his skin color. White people typically recognized that he was a "Negro," but his light-brown skin allowed him to blend in with them in a way that dark-skinned blacks never could.

The ease with which he moved through white society led to family friend Reuben Graham accusing him of "passing for white," though Duncanson clearly appeared to be mixed race. In an 1871 letter to Graham, Duncanson defended himself against the claim that he'd tried to shed his blackness. He suggested not only that he emotionally felt a connection to African Americans but also that he had meaningful relationships with black people. "There

Duncanson's Family

The US census of 1860 reveals that Phoebe Duncanson, the artist's second wife, was his junior by roughly twelve years. She and their children remained in Cincinnati for some years before moving, first to Detroit and then to Seattle, Washington.

Some of Duncanson's descendants still lived in Washington in the 1930s, and pieces of his art have turned up all over the United States.

are colored persons in this city that I love and respect, true and dear to me," he said. "It does not follow that because I am colored that I am bound to kiss every colored or white man I meet.[3]

In the letter, Duncanson declares himself a person of color and proud of it. Still, he refuses to compromise his principles to curry favor with anyone. Had Duncanson snubbed a black person Graham thought he shouldn't have? Was Graham jealous of Duncanson's success? It's unclear what precisely prompted Graham's accusations. The letter suggests that he had spoken badly of Duncanson for a while. Without these details, it's hard to know exactly what to make of the conflict. On the surface, it appears to be about race, but on a deeper level, it was about a complicated relationship between Duncanson and a longtime family friend.

Another reason Duncanson may have hesitated to play up his racial heritage is that he was such an ambitious artist. Emphasizing his blackness likely would have resulted in the art world focusing on his race alone or expecting him to concentrate exclusively on race in his art. But Duncanson didn't wanted to be limited in this way.

Additionally, identifying himself as the first "great black painter" might have earned him the respect of the African American community, but Duncanson was far too humble to have characterized himself that way. He simply felt proud to have had the ability to exhibit his paintings all over the world. In the process, he set a high standard for future black artists to follow.

Today, there's intense interest in the works of early African American painters, and Duncanson's creations

Photographed in 1907, Henry Ossawa Tanner is one of many black artists who benefited from Robert S. Duncanson's legacy.

are no exception. Approximately 250 pieces of his work are still around today, and some of his larger pieces have been auctioned off for six figures. Renewed interest in his work has also led to efforts to honor his legacy. An artist-in-residence program at the Taft Museum of Art bears his name. Also, the *Detroit Free Press* announced in 2018 that Duncanson's grave—unmarked for roughly 150 years after his death—was finally getting a marker. He is buried in the Historic Woodland Cemetery in Monroe, Michigan, where he once lived. His grave marker is made of black granite. It includes the year of his death and his quote, "I have no color on the brain; all I have on the brain is paint."[4]

Chronology

1790

At about this time, Duncanson's grandfather is emancipated from slavery in Virginia and moves north to New York.

1821

Robert Duncanson is born in Fayette, New York.

1828

The Duncanson family moves to Monroe, Michigan.

1838

Robert advertises as part of a house-painting partnership.

1841

He settles in Mount Healthy, near Cincinnati, Ohio. *Sketches of Cincinnati* is published.

1845

The Drunkard's Plight is completed.

1846

A Cincinnati reporter visits Duncanson's home.

1847-1848

Duncanson spends time in Detroit.

1848

Commissioned by the Rev. Charles Avery, Duncanson completes *Cliff Mine*.

1849

He finishes *Blue Hole, Flood Waters, Little Miami River*.

1849-1850

Duncanson paints murals at Belmont, Nicholas Longworth's home.

1851

Duncanson paints *View of Cincinnati*, based on a daguerreotype.

1852

Harriet Beecher Stowe's *Uncle Tom's Cabin* is published in Boston.

1853

Reviewers pan Duncanson's *Uncle Tom and Little Eva*. He departs for Europe.

1854

Duncanson returns to Cincinnati.

1855

Duncanson and J. P. Ball create a traveling exhibit.

1858

Duncanson finishes a full-size portrait of Nicholas Longworth.

1860

Abraham Lincoln is elected president, which increases tensions between the North and the South.

1861

The Civil War begins on April 12 with the Battle of Fort Sumter.

Duncanson finishes *Land of the Lotus Eaters* in the spring; the painting is exhibited in Cincinnati in June.

1862

Duncanson travels through parts of the Midwest and New England.

1863

He and his wife cross the border to Canada.

1863-1865

The artist partners with Canadian photographer William Notman.

1865

He exhibits *Land of the Lotus Eaters* in England, Ireland, and Scotland.

1866

Duncanson returns to Cincinnati.

1868

Duncanson experiments with a new style, painting Scottish subjects and themes.

1870

He finishes *Ellen's Isle* and attempts to give it to Senator Charles Sumner.

1871

Reuben Graham accuses Duncanson of distancing himself from his blackness; the artist angrily responds to this claim.

1872

Duncanson collapses while hanging his paintings in Detroit. He dies on December 21.

1926

Cincinnati historian Wendell P. Dabney sparks new interest in Duncanson's art with the publication of *Cincinnati's Colored Citizens*.

1951

An *Art in America* article by James A. Porter draws new attention to Duncanson's career.

1980

Lost Duncanson letters resurface with the publication of *Robert S. Duncanson: 19th Century Black Romantic Painter*.

1993

Joseph D. Ketner's *The Emergence of the African-American Artist: Robert S. Duncanson* is published.

2011

Thomas Cole National Historic Site exhibits many of Duncanson's landscape paintings.

Chapter Notes

Chapter 1

The Painter and the Poet

1. Robert W. Hill Jr., ed. *Tennyson's Poetry: A Norton Critical Edition* (New York: W.W. Norton, 1999), pp. 76–77.
2. Hill, p. 80.
3. Joseph D. Ketner, *The Emergence of the African-American Artist: Robert S. Duncanson, 1821-1872* (Colombia, MO: University of Missouri Press, 1993), p. 154.
4. Ketner, p. 154.
5. Ketner, p. 155.
6. Wendell P. Dabeny. *Cincinnati's Colored Citizens: Historical, Sociological and Biographical.* (Cincinnati, OH: The Dabney Publishing Company, 1926), p. 91.

Chapter 2

Artisan to Artist

1. James A. Porter, "Robert S. Duncanson: Midwestern Romantic-Realist," *Art in America*, October 1951, pp. 99–154.
2. Joseph D. Ketner, *The Emergence of the African-American Artist: Robert S. Duncanson, 1821-1872* (Colombia, MO: University of Missouri Press, 1993).
3. Lynda Roscoe Hartigan, *Sharing Traditions: Five Black Artists in Nineteenth-Century America* (Washington, DC: Smithsonian Institution Press, 1985), p. 65.
4. Ketner, p. 13.

Chapter 3

An Artist's Growth

1. Charles Cist, *Cincinnati in 1841: Its Early Annals and Future Prospects* (Cincinnati, OH, 1841), p. 13.
2. Cist, p. 42.

3. "Dreadful Tragedy in the Theatre—John Randolph's Slaves—A Negro Artist," *The Liberator*, August 21, 1846.
4. "Dreadful Tragedy in the Theatre—John Randolph's Slaves—A Negro Artist."

Chapter 4

Friends and Patrons

1. James A. Porter, "Robert S. Duncanson: Midwestern Romantic-Realist," *Art in America*, October 1951, p. 121.

Chapter 5

Hudson River School

1. "Robert S. Duncanson," Smithsonian American Art Museum, retrieved April 27, 2019, https://americanart.si.edu/artist/robert-s-duncanson-1353.
2. James A. Porter, "Robert S. Duncanson: Midwestern Romantic-Realist," *Art in America*, October 1951, p. 121.

Chapter 6

Becoming a Master

1. Romare Bearden and Harry Henderson, *A History of African-American Artists from 1792 to the Present*, (New York: Pantheon Books, 1993), p. 28.
2. Joseph D. Ketner, *The Emergence of the African-American Artist: Robert S. Duncanson, 1821-1872* (Colombia, MO: University of Missouri Press, 1993).

Chapter 7

International Acclaim

1. James A. Porter, "Robert S. Duncanson: Midwestern Romantic-Realist," *Art in America*, October 1951, p. 136.

Chapter 8

Highland Overtones

1. Joseph D. Ketner, *The Emergence of the African-American Artist: Robert S. Duncanson, 1821-1872* (Colombia, MO: University of Missouri Press, 1993).

Chapter 9

Sad Demise

1. James A. Porter, "Robert S. Duncanson: Midwestern Romantic-Realist," *Art in America*, October 1951, p. 102.
2. Porter, p. 145.
3. James Dallas Parks, *Robert S. Duncanson:19th Century Black Romantic Painter* (Washington, DC: The Association Publishers, 1980).
4. Ryan Patrick Hooper, "Pioneering Black Artist Robert S. Duncanson Will Finally Get Tombstone," *Detroit Free Press*, September 30, 2018, https://www.freep.com/story/entertainment/arts/2018/09/30/african-american-artist-robert-duncanson-grave/1452886002.

Glossary

ambiguous Vague or unclear; not one thing or the other.

cherubic Angelic, especially in a childlike way.

commission To hire a person to complete a job or a project.

countenance One's face or facial expression.

daguerreotype A picture taken by an old photographic process that used iodine and mercury.

induce To bring something about or cause something to happen.

intoxicate To make drunk.

misconception The wrong idea; a misinformed idea.

plight Situation or predicament, typically a difficult one.

premier The best or the top.

revere To admire, worship, or hold in high regard.

scythe A cutter, pruner, or machete-like object.

transient Fleeting, moving from place to place.

unprecedented The first time something has happened.

virulent Very fierce, hostile, or harsh.

Further Reading

BOOKS

Dabney, Wendell P. *Cincinnati's Colored Citizens: Historical, Sociological and Biographical*. Cincinnati, OH: The Dabney Publishing Company, 1926.

Hartigan, Lynda Roscoe. *Sharing Traditions: Five Black Artists in Nineteenth-Century America*. Washington, DC: Smithsonian Institution Press, 1985.

Hill, Robert W., Jr., ed. *Tennyson's Poetry: A Norton Critical Edition*. New York: W.W. Norton, 1999.

Lubin, David M. *Picturing a Nation: Art and Social Change in Nineteenth-Century America*. New Haven, CT: Yale University Press, 1994.

Taylor, Henry Louis, Jr. *Race and the City: War, Community, and Protest in Cincinnati, 1820-1970*. Urbana, IL: University of Illinois Press, 1993.

WEBSITES

Robert S. Duncanson: Cincinnati Art Museum

https://artsandculture.google.com/exhibit/NQJyYinFqXw_Lw

Google Arts and Culture features a biography of the artist and a collection of his work.

Robert S. Duncanson: LACMA Collections

https://collections.lacma.org/node/165519

The artist's webpage at the Los Angeles County Museum of Art includes a biographical sketch and an image of an early still life.

Index

Charlotte Etinde-Crompton

Samuel Willard Crompton

About the Authors

Charlotte Etinde-Crompton was born and raised in Zaire and came to Massachusetts at the age of twenty. Her artistic sensibility stems from her early exposure to the many talented artists of her family and tribe, which include master woodcarvers. She developed an interest in African American art after arriving in the United States.

Samuel Willard Crompton is a tenth-generation New Englander who now lives in metropolitan Atlanta. He was a history professor at Holyoke Community College for twenty-eight years. His interest in the arts comes from his woodcarver father and his oil-painter mother. Crompton is the author and editor of many books, including a number of nonfiction young adult titles with Enslow Publishing.